hazard or fall

CATHERINE HALES

hazard or fall

Shearsman Books
Exeter

First published in the United Kingdom in 2010 by
Shearsman Books Ltd
58 Velwell Road
Exeter EX4 4LD

www.shearsman.com

ISBN 978-1-84861-113-9
First Edition

Acknowledgements

Many of these poems have previously appeared, some in an earlier form, in:
*Brittle Star, Coffee House Poetry, Fire, Gists and Piths, Great Works, Haiku
Quarterly, Litter, Neon Highway, Orbis, Poetry Salzburg Review, Shadow
Train, Shearsman, Stride, Tears in the Fence.*

Thanks are due to the editors.

Cover photograph copyright © Alex Nikada, 2009.

CONTENTS

unearthings

"everything we see could also be otherwise"
          —ludwig wittgenstein,

"the ship was travelling so to speak along the line
that divides what we can perceive from what
nobody has yet seen"
          —w g sebald

"painting has the power to point the finger at what
happened"
          —fernando botero

seeing it through

a quiet astringent compromise of sorts—
it's surely the meek who suffer, several see
the dovetailing of memory into the brickwork, while
new debts are expunged by the needy
mellifluous panic of a dawn chorus in the distance
ascending from bare ruin'd notions of the
bone, the idle & the clinamen. & finding this
in the sort of seedy restaurant that serves
unwholesome pastimes on the internet, no doubt
there'll be consequences, & nothing would surprise
in a time of manifestos & mellow fruitfulness.
bringing forward the attenuated circumstance
of unrequited séances, the overall effect
may bewilder the uncertain, the queasy,
the flavour of the season. & various
of their majesties may even attend the play
in soporific wonder though the span be meagre.

how, then, best to serve the appetite? a pre-dawn
vertical insertion event with incontinent
ordnance? that would do the trick to swell
a scene or two & send the orderlies running
for the wings. but is it to be trusted, things
being not quite as they seem? a new
menu item with an icon on the screen
horrifies with auguries of germ warfare
if not nipped in the code & sharpish—o brave
new world that has such weasels in it. & where
are the artefacts likely to be seen? a drifting cloud
is just a drifting cloud; either situation
is ugly, but one of them will be necessary—
the governance of profiteroles depends on it;

until in the presence of the ineffable they squander
what resistance they've afforded to the wild,
sarcastic narks surrounding the citadel. wholly
to blame, & trusting to the power of integers,
the creatures crawl into their caverns & expire.

interims

temporary lodging

as good a place as any   where the book
just falls open   mid-sentence   to start
here   & subvert the order   far

from the madding   & hardly
a stone standing   cities we'd imagined
way off the beaten   the word is out

let's follow that as far as it'll take us
to the edge where even the largest continent
crumbles   how do we bear this

awakening   here   where you come from
you told me once   before the noise begins
at first light you can hear the lions in the zoo

all over the city   you cried remembering
here at least the windows are watertight
for the time being   we can take our chance

relocation

sharing stories   for this time at least
a common thread   our minatory arguments
will ensnare us   as the seesaw of seasons
swings again   tilts towards expansion
of all our desires   we stand at the window
(across blank fields our light   a beacon
deer blink & cough)   what I mean to say

waking early in this house   the night shifts
haunts   accretions bringing home absence

moving on   from room to room   to get the measure
of this available space   & the day approaching
our breath misting   time to grasp   rearrange
whatever roots have survived the freeze

threshold

a sogging drawl   where the body's
syntax is wiped from the map   different elements
compete for the mind   contours shift
boundaries I'd no longer want
to negotiate
                    where can I go
camping out for now   between languages
hoping at least for a good night's sleep
& perchance   that liminal place of dreaming

an autumnal surrey lane   a gospel hall
smelling of damp and old age   my mother's in there
with the others   they're arranging
the harvest festival   & start singing
a hymn   a happiness I can't share
at the door   looking in   looking out

the choices we make   the fibs we try
to avoid   & at last   the mind is clearer
the further away   the closer

just here for the ride

a place to start from   or end up   this far
from   say   the sea   the various paths
that have led to this conjunction   & here

the versions part   one myth's as good
as any other   though none allows for difference
they terrify   but give you a head start

I am not one of those who named the stars
& imagined them into constellations   I do not have
the certainty of a fish   a rock   a lotus

I'm left with an unreadable sky   stories
waiting for the retelling   it's what I see
along the way that makes the journey worthwhile

open road

this journey   somewhere between

now at least   (whipping through landscapes
with fields and trees   munching cows
grubby sheep   horses moving fast)

and that's real   (clouds
the colour of a bruise behind a line of poplars
a glimpse of a hawk circling high)

how it all fits together   neatly
this syntax

travelogue

places   stations
just passing through   always
on the move

***

miles to go   and then the storm
that caught us by surprise
remember
how we sat it out
how the rain
blanked out the mountains
how while we were away
the landscape changed completely
cutting off our retreat
the waterlogged engine
forced us to change our plans
nothing for it but to take
what we could and head
for the high pass
leaving things behind
like clouds ripping softly among pines

***

where we set out from   like a vivid
dream forgotten on awakening   is the dream
less real than the awakening into
here and now   where we'll be
years from now

***

heaving heaps of dark   daring
to put a name to it
get beyond   distance unbridgeable
by any stretch of the imagination

***

surrounded by a language
I wasn't born to   I've mastered it
rather well   but always
there's the hint of an accent
a misplaced intonation
that betrays

***

mirrors   meetings
setting an edge
where we'd be   no-
body   just pure image
to be able to say this
is my hacceity
myself on the way
returning

***

knowing I've dreamt   try to reenter
revisit stations I've passed through
finding them disjunctive like when I
try to say me   the picture's cranky
slightly misty   out of sync   as though
through thick glass   like dreaming   I was here
but I was someone else   the more
I try to see the more I recede
like looking through the shrinking end
of a telescope   try to reenter
the dream   it's gone   but I carry it
like a forgotten bus ticket at the bottom of my bag

***

which way now   mapping the terrain
as I go

***

and there   the meaning
that's eluded us   a risky leap
away   resplendent
teasing   fata morgana
that's it   light
glancing off the wing of a kingfisher
diving

driving through norfolk

i.m. max sebald

in a hired car   london to norwich
on the old A11   returning under cover
of a dense night after all these years

this is the landscape he died in
on my birthday on a journey like this
he and I both emigrants   I remember
his gentle allgäu accent his sardonic smile
under his moustache   warm searching eyes
our lives crossed like the shadow
of a bird in flight

out there the massive darkness sliding past
a continent without maps

interims   alone with the dark
the feeling of dizziness begins behind the eyes
the nausea comes later
I seem to have slipped into that space
where all is abeyance   bridging time
in remembered landscapes

my headlights brush ahead
bone fingers groping for the road
silvering worn brick   blackthorn   oak
coming at me like phantoms
from another landscape   familiar words
pronounced askew

I slacken speed into the curve
entering a sleeping village
permanent as ploughshares

a pub   houses   edging back
the last streetlight

I have somehow become extrinsic
a random point of light
sealed up with the words I'd use
to name and define the vastness
momentarily bright
as the rings of saturn

geography

the old maps won't do
ditch-
water of the mind

*

our landscapes rip
and crumple
and where are we?

*

when we are most lost
we think
we know where we are

*

boundaries confound
we're hard put
to see where they should be

*

is the darkest place
in the middle
or right off the edge?

*

it's a matter of scale
the closer you get
the more exact the lie

low tide at burnham overy staithe (february)

still point of the year
we here   the silence of the place
embarrasses to whispers   our voices

echoing in mist
between the harbour and the dunes
boats left to lean into mud

behind us the land flattened
under grey light
the causeway across salt marsh

ahead sand   somewhere sea
a gradual transition of nuances
how far we have come

to the blurred edge   land and sea
cease to define   and we
suddenly ankle-deep in it

in each other

divination

signs   drenched in meaning   early
dew   and another fine   but maybe

later cloud   shudders like a headache
lightning   it'll pass   where

were we then   ah yes   the signs
we were seeking   the words to tell

score

streets after rain   how the air
changes key   modulation
back to major   scherzo

take it as it comes   this day's
haphazard   ragged scraps of cloud
between showers   the next downpour's
darkening for   here it comes

what I'd want to say   meaning implicit
in the *how*   now I'm scrabbling
rearrange for sense   the nerve   alive to

small comfort

"only the wind counts for the poet"
(marina tsvetaeva)

how the storm runs amok with us—
in the early hours we wake

listen to the wind
scouring out the streets

toppling dustbins in the *hof*
screaming in our guttering

glad of the small protection
of walls windows and a roof

we huddle closer to what we have
only words to offer

words and simply being here
sensing the danger in holding on

first day of spring

when the ice melted
they saw the corpse in the water

they rolled it over with sticks
pulled it half out

prodded the bloated limbs
the eyelids drying stretched open in the sun

but if they expected a resurrection
there was none

in the name of

& when faith seems so much like a failure
to live   & the procession moves on   to finish
fireworks   of course   & the damage left

sticks & stones may break my   remember
but words can never   places   we'd put up with
the mind's collateral   taken together   alone

in a yurt somewhere   savouring how sand
scours at the subtle lies we live by   bones
aren't even the half of it   on the march

revelation

shadows angle away
the sky invades
wherever you look
there are roofs   balconies
awash with it

harsh light pointing up
to perfection the paint
peeling from walls
unswept corners   cracks
blemishes   unwanted hair

were we to believe
in some deity we'd say
this is all
the evidence we need
of divine revelation

even dogs slacken down around midday
when nothing else matters
at least we have this
the thrill of inflicting
the wound of silence

incident involving swans
& a poem by w.b. yeats

the insistency of their wingbeats
punctuates the afternoon   their coming
makes me look up from my book

a sudden blow   the great wings beating still

& follow their flight   wingtip to wingtip
precise as pilots   steady as steel
between the banks   beneath the bridge

at some signal   so it seems   they stop
tilt their wings to cup the rush of air
their *dark webs* sluice the surface   & they're down

in a soft explosion   I can't hear
at this distance   amid this chatter
& my milchkaffee getting cold

the broken wall the burning roof and tower and agamemnon dead

the afternoon regroups   I find my place   around
back in mid-sentence   its mythologies   as though
nothing were more mundane than that landing

sightlines

portrait of

allowing for the limning of a likeness   light's
evolution in the retina   the object   love

the desire for love   or its likeness   principles
of being   with this fall of the light   here

now   sequence this as you will   there's no
design   make it mean   the world you see

scored into the margins of the manuscript
woven into its illuminated capitals   sneaking in

details of a life beyond the text   mundane
complete   down to the necessary flaw

than venice

by the waters of   sofas empty bottles plastic bags full of
with a skinful of myself I just like to walk on my own if that's

the shriek of swifts dropping through air &
the photographer starts by painting the model's body

the archaeological record's real   all our mythology's
ariel awol & caliban in his soul   stale bread &

small pools caught in fists of petals   disposal
fronts propelled by trenches of pressure   accumulating

until she's invisible against the brickwork   all this at my
take another look at   yes & some of it lands in the

narratives

out of terracotta hills   free-
wheeling down to dry valleys   even

roads   villages where facades conceal centuries
of untold bruising   the normal rigmarole

we're too preoccupied to notice   whizzing through
sniffing the earthiness up ahead   the darkening

a sprung gust upsets our equilibrium
but not for long   here's a rustic taverna   chianti

& pasta   & postcards   sitting it out while the storm
fractures a perfect day until we can carry on

original condition

puzzling   the way ahead   these pedestrian concerns
filling in   & still connecting to   the river is a straight line

to a spire between trees   & then the long walk further out
a breeze off the sea from the east   wind worrying waves

to a frenzy   & in spite of   like a picture postcard
& an ideal package for a day out   away from

& not having to think of   but hard work   this I didn't
bargain for   mark it down as a shrewd move   take stock

words in retreat   changing tack to accommodate
prevailing vagaries   read the small print

factoring in

the way the sun slants into the street   a routine
to lean into   pythagorean in its simplicity

plus ou moins l'infini   with prices through the roof
the line so elegantly drawn   exclusive rights

fortunes lost   & bonuses made regardless
(the clowns are tumbling in the street   don't

weep)   candles will be dear this winter
& traders come down to pasture   future's

worth a bet   it's in the air   with a payload of gilt-
edged   be daft not to   & feeling it's half the trick

context

the clarity of the thought   present
tense   where were the water gods when

we needed them   still & translucent
perfectly packaged residue of artefacts

nor plagued with notions of propriety
paralysed   the splash obfuscated by its

sudden contingency   allowing her at least
the veracity of a slingback   wanton

hooves across halogen flora   the arch-
aeological record is real   it can't lie she said

on balance

a certain seepage will always occur
from meaning   the best metaphors not

always the best insurance   secure
all you want behind plate glass

with infrared sensors et cetera   worth
a bomb   a mask (example)   making

death eternal   you know   the thing you
fine dust of   test for fingerprints

then set up road blocks   it's when
you part your lips that the problems begin

war on

commercial pressures illuminating the   why
have a thousand gods when one is one

too many   the borders are porous   you're out
there somewhere she said poking her finger at the

man with a green parrot on his arm gets into the s-bahn
deconstruction of an eye   cornea   retina

for public consumption   the facts are
mapping our fears on to a face in the paper

in the hittite capital the correspondence of empires
a system of cisterns that still functions today

field walking

the first steps are to acclimatise the eye   to look for
the hand-fashioned planes & edges   & distinguish them

from accidental fractures from slanting blows
of the plough   be prepared for disappointment

not every field will yield a crop of artefacts   not even
a single slim flint arrowhead to slip in your pocket   if it's

excitement & great discoveries & gold you're after you'd best
join indiana jones or lara croft or get a book on howard carter

the most you'll find here is a sharpened hand-axe that probably
once smashed someone's skull   wear stout shoes

megalithic

graves that were ancient even before teutons began
inflecting their verbs   nothing much to see in passing

just boulders dumped by scandinavian glaciers   but these
were passages to an afterlife   neolithic chieftains

newly powerful   in possession of livestock   stone axes
wives   buried with all their wealth & status intact

in a landscape that seems depleted now   soil skimmed off
axes in museums   megaliths ornamenting churchyards   is

this the hereafter they were in such awe of   she picks up three
acorns from a six hundred year old oak   drops them in her bag

.

agnostic

flying fish fore & aft & alongside   but she was hoping
for a sighting of dolphins   to let her believe

more abstruse stories   running from side to side
of ferries' decks   her eyes stringent   she reeled in

spray and meltemi   passing patmos the sea
was calmer but still no glimpse of those mythical

silk black backs   on her flight home she sat next to
someone who claimed he'd seen dolphins   he'd been

fishing he said & they came in frolicking round his boat
almost near enough to touch   simply there

a fortnight before full moon

the kitchen being the heart of things   she likes
to eat the loaf crusts   (but always asks if I mind)

tulips wilting   the glaze on the vase crazed
no more circumlocutions   circumventions   where

did I put my   placing too much   trusting in
blindly   is the hypotenuse always the quickest

such comfort in reducing everything to theorems
even distance   aldebaran is bright   there's mars

in the next room I lie awake   squaring up for
a favourable transit   incalculable conjunction

reconnaissance

this is what we know   all our tracking
syntax revealing build-up in the hills   all

our semantic maps aligned to alchemy   pixel
expansion in the subcutaneous zone   satnav

carefully positioned for the imminent takeaway
(a few stray nouns need reining in)   mis-

understanding rife in the erogenous seats
synchronising clocks for perfect control   for

ease of operation please do not adjust your
cranial space mimetic fingertips skin temperature

representing

this is how things are   buildings leaning
scattily in the wind   burnt at edges

discarded shoes littering the bloodstained ground
& vision dying out with a whimper at the van-

ishing point at the back of perspective   still
life   meaning strung like wires between opposite

poles   spasms between us   who think we know   lost
in translation   what we see in the mirror is not

what we get   that structure is only bones after all
& a palette of ochres reds yellows blues   titanium white

art of the detective

forensics will chivvy a better tale   but for now
we're stuck with the evidence of our own eyes

investigating the tiniest details   trajectories
it's all indicative   you just can't trust   the how of the crime

but never the why   like microscoping single threads of a canvas
splashed with a random idea of colour   all our training

militates against stepping back to see the greater whole
the conditional aspect   the adjacent dreams   involving

less & less of anything we can find to reconstruct   the trick
is not to lose that while coming in close for certainty

at the scene

integral to the larceny perpetrated on hair
roots & colouration in mid-stream

first thing in the morning she'll find out
& wanting to know where all this came from

the slow sun sliding off the side of the aircraft
descending & pertinent to the argument is the point

of view of the observer   & taking into account
the imminent closure of the airport she

hangs her hypotheses out to dry on the count-
less blades of grass illuminating mimicry

winter morning

the sky's illuminated blue   the vast shadow
of a pigeon before it alights on the ridge over a window

a pink balloon perhaps pursuing a miniature number six
comes bouncing into sight around the corner on the cobbles

the light carving everything into sharp relief
cars passing   in spite of this   the stillness

of dark windows   this is where   keeping vigil
it's possible to pass days in silence   hardly looking out

scraping parchment & starting again   sharpening
feathers to the point of flight   & holding back

divergences

to be among them   the red buildings
red brick in the sinking light   & in them

rooms glowing gold in reflected light
from wooden floors   uncluttered white walls

a winter's gravity   & dispassion   as of
equations proving a parallel universe

brushing my cheek with its wind   or that I can cup
in my hand and toss   but never see   only mind

can conceive   when freezing may well happen
wind scissor in from the arctic   snow deaden

across the

singularities out there sucking light   so many
laid the foundation for a face-to-face

grinding millet   lighting fires   the tip of the mountain
outrageous to award a free kick for   where did I hear

a shopping mall is now a lifestyle center
the woman walked out into the water weighted

from the window we could see rising from a bed of cloud
its beam marking the sands   if we set out now

waves increasing frequency   he went supernova
deep into the present   mint   crushed cumin

in the nature of

striations crust the livid blue of the proposition
how the hell is the simplest form of the answer

this is the way we came obviating the need
to go back there   strictures line the road

with little bits of paper   that celebratory moment
as we emerge from   & here the narrative falters

resisting its own homogeneity   the geiger counter
begins to crackle as the man on the radio

nears a hot spot in the evacuated zone   he says
he likes local variation in the dialects of birdsong

precautionary

what's in this year (though nothing new)   made
in china   the aleatory fall of light

on a crumbling wall   more authentic than the real thing
in uncertain times we turn to interpretations

of the past to avoid the necessity of facing a future
of unknown provenance   the earthquake (7.6

on the richter scale) struck with devastating force
before leaving I check that all the rituals

have been observed   beschwichtigung
der häuslichen götter   take a last look & lock the door

out of time

the directives are ambiguous   leading to
the sightline out of this building   she

can't quite decide   the direction taken
in these photos   hazard or fall   & not

knowing when to stop could prove disastrous
seventeen seconds until the bell goes & all

hell's let loose   motion detected in the chamber
expressed in opaque officialese   while you're here

there's not much time to master the essentials
please take your litter with you when you leave

unearthings

for all eternity

I

implosive inscriptions   fuel tanks
full & ready for the long haul   holding
companies to take the strain
on tv mr seen the graffiti sprayer
who's evaded capture for thirty years

in whatever language   a keynote speech
a system change   a jostling of regimes
about a common axis
the bestial stench
of ammonia   piss & shit of a million bats

initials gouged into soft red school brick
the river stacked with memorabilia
the lights of various beasts
faulty propositions
regarding the passing of time

during commercial breaks   the process
between the aim & the achievable   the chair
she sat in with a palette knife
surrounded by mirrors and the angels
she painted   adorning walls & corridors

to one side a passage led to two
smaller chambers   in the mornings
coffee black no sugar   a slice
of toast with fine-cut marmalade
the stench in the tomb is still unbearable

II

that being said is negotiable   rosemary
growing on her balcony   there will be wars
she says over resources
the like of which has
never been seen before   the body is not

a conventional narrative   erosions &
a metamorphous use of colour   distance was
hard to estimate because
our route was haphazard
loopy   forty years of neglect & now

the bulldozers moving in   dimensions
of a brick unchanged since mohenjo daro
anticipatory compliance
& a fox crossing the road
at midnight   almond blossom & the air

bearing a chill   the motion & the slackening
of motion   revelation of senses to come to
recoding the place
where history left the map
& what we fake revealing what we value

keeping time

the year's full circle
temperatures below measure
our movements   our days

frost at the window
staves and bars blank of anything
but this distorting

whiteness   out at the edge
of the city there's ice on the lakes
the forest shakes free

a cluster of crows
black crotchets inked against
the unstaved sky

and then the coming home
mid-city   a new fall of snow
in our courtyard

crystallised air holds
our music in abeyance
for the time of thaw

quantum sonnet

the non-relation of points in space; yet
the very fact of their existence posits
some sort of relationship, even if
it is to ignore each other completely. such is

the bravura of a simple life, attracting
the kind of criticism that tends to come
with the territory; the macchiavellian turn
without the sweetener of a smile across the table;

surrendering to the dumb logic of symbols
scored in stone; & the existential need
to exorcise ghosts, especially those in boxes.

god is like schroedinger's cat, you say,
& point to the play of light across the wall;
the door closing with some degree of grace

dereliction of

not exactly frivolous   she holds
such antics in abeyance   the body's
convoluted autonomy   concave as
except as otherwise   spontaneous
a stance   a shell of artifice
to shield this fragile skin
panic setting in with the in
tensity of doorways   intricate
retaliations flirt among
these tectonic shifts   these
multiple channels   a sign to whom
& whereas the parties   keeping it
under wraps   down on the street
the word is out   she spits on her image

what's for pudding

instant whip the fervent dream of masochist
& sadist alike buying into the whole
crepuscular transaction but only while stocks last
don't be disappointed the thing is unlike
any other thing & so without compare
a light breeze holding its own among
massed equestrian statues symphony of a thousand
supermarket trolleys streets blocked off in the
centre & all the exits sealed she
runs her hands over carious stone here
in these railway arches are bullet holes
the flag over the bundestag bought &
paid for & for dessert this sweet
insubstantial stuff to satisfy this fundamental need

marginalia

who writes that sort of thing by hand any more
it's a short step from that to putting it all aside
for a pocketful of buy two get one free & who
can say whether this is just incompetence
or the result of a well-thought-out strategy
the subtext being as it's always been an improvement
on last year's menu & improvisation as a means
of placing hand on heart & aching for authentic
melodrama complete with mandolins
& all the trimmings the offer stands please
read carefully it's wholly inappropriate
a crispy base just like in the restaurant
I'm not sure where all this is leading but I like
the punctuation you may tick more than one box

in transit

we'd expected a few hold-ups but nothing like
this choke of traffic backed up to the border
it's not all doom & gloom you know & breaking
news & palimpsests & clearing misconceptions
the air-conditioning on the blink & then
the lack of running water we didn't deserve
where can we put our trust if not in the power
of broken stones plaintive spaces & public
declarations we apologise for any in
convenience due to disruptions to services moving
forward we set our goals high we're setting standards
in quality & price judge us by our results
for account information please press one for your
security this conversation is being recorded

road kill

arterial infractions spillage of imagining
what you look like after hearing your voice
on the radio the houses collapsed into a hole
in the ground medieval chalk pits no-one knew
were there they weren't marked on any map we
were plonked down in the middle of nowhere & told
to find our own way back some were never
heard from again multiple fractures &
concussion & there were people taking pictures
even before the police & ambulance arrived
they listen to the frequencies how toxic
well we wouldn't want it getting into the ground
water white noise after five hours both carriage
ways cleared diversion ahead get in lane

subject to

the lines are made to work hard & yet
are totally imaginary stepping off the boat
& handing my coin to the ferryman I realise
that this isn't where I want to be at all
& the ferryman's refusing to take me back imagine
things really having the thick black outline we draw
them with to define contain divide & own
without recourse to the usual methodologies
the courts overstretched & it'll take several months
even to get a hearing the improbability drive
cranked up to maximum there's some poor bugger
outside the door says he's been summonsed doesn't
have a clue what he's supposed to have done the portrait's
cleverly painted the eyes follow you wherever you go

heavy weather

condition stable   since we know
our narrators can't be trusted
in fact they wobble quite a lot & that's
today in a crowded market at the busiest
proposals for an international ban on
respectively the manner of its conception
reported heavier-than-expected second-quarter
it was only afterwards that she   came down
in a residential area in the suburbs   our
preliminary analysis is confirming that
could be applied to producing   documents
left on a train   the forgery was undetectable
except for the age of the paper   a ridge of high
necessities of waiting   continuing fine

contingent on

the wilful savaging of string quartets when
was the last time ice formed over the lakes
& even in august you'd be surprised prime
numbers are the key of course & prime
time tv the place for maximum exposure
unearthings of artefacts & fragments the ruined faces
of card players in a painting & ships that foundered
on rocks on the scillies thinking they were some-
where else entirely & hence the need for a method
for determining longitude down by the canal
people playing boules wasps crawling into
coffee cups you're not recording this are you
this is off the record mostly harmless though there are
trouble spots syntax integral to an understanding of

anatomy

understanding the mechanics of say a smile
begins with the bones   bones are
the body's grammar   the rules
that hold it all together   more or less
unbendable   getting harder as we get older
and more brittle   an accidental fracture
or careless blow a fall like a split infinitive
resets and becomes the norm   between
the official version and what the doctor sees
is a certain flexibility   it's for those
always younger than us to see how far
bones will bend

                        but bones alone
will not move   cannot get themselves
to the top of the stairs   they need the body's
vocabulary nouns and verbs layers
of muscle tendons fat skin glands and organs
follicles hairs fingernails blood flowing
in a net of veins saliva sweat
the gap between the toes where dirt collects
thoughts made flesh   but when
wounds heal the scars can change
meanings entirely   and when
the language is forgotten it's just so much
meat on the slab

                    is there any part
that can't be touched and broken
the mind perhaps that sets it all in motion
the idioms that articulate the flesh to move the bones
cleave the brain and still it can't be seen   there are
more subtle ways than straightforward violence like
mass circulation to impose
and reinforce a dialect   or bright lights
or locked and darkened rooms or simply
being alive in the twenty-first century   and so
getting back to what I was saying   I value
idiolect   that particular turn of phrase   the way
you turn your head just so
when you smile

dimensions of

nicking
bone on the way to

stillness
shifting blocks of

dark
spaces   between

in the rest of light
the mind perceiving this

whole
figures in the

midst
white

stirring of   protrudes
into the room

the sentence
hard to target

a word's
sima

beyond
reach of

shift &
sigil

gravid
engraved

fitting the spaces
so well

ideas of
words

being the sheer
effect of

& the outcome
travels

obfuscation   benthic
you'll see   a thought

chimeras   beached up
petals   medusa

boughing   after the felt
nothing   explosion

happens   & slight tsunami
here   takes shape

slippage of   movement
shipwreck   of imaginary

false   capital
beacons   nuclear

the long journey   instability
of excrement   at subatomic

from open field   particle
to sea   level

catching on   wind
drift   rearranging

a viable   body's
alter   limits

native to   picked
place   bones   this

snagging the mind's   photograph is
fence   genuine

directed   dark
into a room   & this

with a certain   is what
vagueness   matters

words   holding it all
a mere hint   together

of what's   tugging
before our eyes   at mind

as defined by   theories of
fire   string &

& from the ruins   membrane   only
phoenix   mind

feeding on   can conceive
picked bones   each word its own

myth of   big   (so to speak)
mind   bang

& the word is   background
a pall of black smoke   like tinnitus

traces of bone &   or keeping
artefact   the rhythm

in a layer   going
of sand   a backbeat

a fastness   a   borrowed
sense of affinity   syntax

veils of light
& dark

matter
torn

away   beyond
perspective

still
more

lingering
in the comfy

warmth
of meanings

that won't
the last guests

clinging to
empty glasses